EXCEPTIONAL YOU

Refusing a Life of Average

Judy L. Smith, Ph.D.

WESTBOW
PRESS®
A DIVISION OF THOMAS NELSON
& ZONDERVAN

WestBow Press books may be ordered through booksellers or by contacting:

WestBow Press
A Division of Thomas Nelson & Zondervan
1663 Liberty Drive
Bloomington, IN 47403
www.westbowpress.com
1 (866) 928-1240

Because of the dynamic nature of the Internet, any web addresses or links contained in this book may have changed since publication and may no longer be valid. The views expressed in this work are solely those of the author and do not necessarily reflect the views of the publisher, and the publisher hereby disclaims any responsibility for them.

Any people depicted in stock imagery provided by Thinkstock are models, and such images are being used for illustrative purposes only. Certain stock imagery © Thinkstock.

ISBN: 978-1-5127-1022-9 (sc)
ISBN: 978-1-5127-1023-6 (hc)
ISBN: 978-1-5127-1021-2 (e)

Library of Congress Control Number: 2015914042

Print information available on the last page.

WestBow Press rev. date: 10/08/2015

Contents

Dedication

*T*his book is dedicated to my Heavenly Father, who taught me through His Word that I can do and have everything that I desire. He has also put within me the determination to flow always in the spirit of excellence.

I also dedicate this book to my life-long friend Anita D. Wilmott, who has always encouraged and inspired me to perform at optimum in everything I do. Thank you so much Ann for your words of wisdom, encouragement and for your unending support. Your friendship is priceless.

Acknowledgement

I acknowledge and thank my loving husband, best friend, confidant and pastor, Apostle Dr. C. Clifford Smith, III, for his covering, patience, love and support. Thank you for allowing me the time to write this book. Thank you also for encouraging me to be exceptional in all I do. I love and appreciate you deeply.

Introduction

$\mathcal{L}$ife is full of possibilities and awesome potential. Opportunities are only a short reach away. God has planned a great life for us, but so many never choose the path of His will. Some fail to cooperate with His plan and others never get close enough to him to find out what his plan for them is. However, there are those who understand that they do not have to choose to be ordinary, grab on to life with enthusiasm and optimism. What makes the difference?

Individuals who have learned how to live at the level of exceptional, have discovered happiness, fulfillment and contentment. They make the most out of where they are now and push toward moving from one accomplishment to another. They refuse to remain in a state of dormancy and complacency. They never allow themselves to be held back. You can do the same. Despite challenges, you can be that exceptional person.

You do not have to go through life with your head hung down or focus on the negative. There is no reason to feel inferior or inadequate. You do not have to allow negative persons to dictate to you, making you feel less than. You can be the awesome, wonderful person God created you to be. You have to choose to be great. Through wisdom and determination you can step unto the level of exceptional: a level of joy and satisfaction.

You do not have to dwell in the world of "I will never be...," or "Maybe one day I will..." You have the power and ability to become who you're supposed to, now. No one knows what tomorrow holds, but we can make today work in our favor.

In this book, you will discover how to become that exceptional person. You will find simple, yet profound steps to assist you in your quest for an exceptional life. Through these steps you will focus your vision and improve you thinking and outlook of life. I believe that if you use these steps, you will ultimately come into a place of empowerment and exceptional living for the rest of your life.

In *Exceptional You,* you will discover how to:

- Understand Your Purpose
- Reprogram Your Mind
- Change Your Way of Speaking
- Start Looking Ahead
- Create a Happy and Fulfilled Life

Each of these areas is designed to help get you to that place of 'exceptional' through simple and practical information and suggestions.

You may have experienced the life of low self-esteem and negative mindset all your life. Maybe you know nothing more than failures and heartaches. Perhaps you believed that your life will always be same old ordinary one. But today is your day for a new start and the beginning of a life that is greater than you have ever imagined.

In this book, you will be challenged to push beyond where you have always been, into an arena of blessings, favor and the good life. You will learn that *ordinary* is not a part of your DNA. You may have to go through a time of mindset detoxification, but I believe in you, like God does, that you can and will make it.

I hope that you are ready to become that exceptional Individual. Let's get you started on your journey.

PART ONE

Find Your Purpose

CHAPTER ONE

❀

Understand Your Purpose

As a counselor and mentor, persons often ask me the question, "How do I know what my purpose is?" Knowing your purpose is vital if you are to achieve greatness and become the exceptional person you should. Not knowing or not having a clear understanding of your purpose will cause you to live a life of 'hitting and missing.' This kind of life brings much frustration and disappointments.

Before you can understand your purpose, you must first discover what it is. I did not discover my purpose as early as I would have liked to. For a long time, I had no clue that knowing my purpose was even important. I only knew that something was missing from my life, and I was searching. Later, I realized that the searching was for my purpose. Although I had a number of achievements, I was not satisfied or fulfilled until I discovered why I exist. I discovered that I got so much joy and fulfillment in helping others find their way in life. I love to help them come to the realization that they have worth. It is so wonderful to see people come to that understanding that they can be everything that God intends for them to be. I knew that I had discovered my purpose.

Each of us has been born with a purpose. If we are to discover our purpose, we must consult the Creator. Even before we were born, God had plans for our lives. He has the blueprint by which to pattern our lives. When in doubt, all we have do, is ask him. He wants us to know and understand our purpose and will reveal it to us if we ask. He does not want us to spend years wondering why we exist or what we are supposed to do. He wants us to know why we exist so that we can have a productive and fruitful life.

We have been created by God, and He seeks to have an intimate relationship with Him. You must allow Him to show you what He wants you to do. You must understand why you were created.

Establishing relationship with God is vital to understanding your purpose. Not having a relationship with God, will cause you to seek to fulfill your purpose out of wrong motives. As you become more intimate with God, He will reveal to you what he wants. It is God who has chosen your purpose in life. It is not up for negotiation. He is not going to change his purpose for your life just because you want him to. He intends for you to fulfill that purpose.

When we purchase a piece of equipment, the manufacturer's instructions are always packaged with it. The instructions help us to understand the purpose of the machine, how to assemble it and what it is capable of doing. Usually, the instructions include a warning section. This section explains in detail, the dangers we face if the equipment is not used for the purpose or in the manner for which it was made.

Like the equipment, we too have to be clear about why we exist, so that we can avoid certain pitfalls. Not understanding your purpose can cause you to waste a whole lot of time. You will find yourself pursuing dreams and goals that are unfulfilling. These unfulfilled dreams and goals, cause us often to become frustrated and disillusioned. God holds the master plan for our lives. It is He who gave us the gifts, talents, ambitions and personality that we have. God wants to fulfill our purpose by understanding who we are. He knows that life is meaningless when we have no purpose. He expects us to enjoy our lives.

I know people who have achieved highly and experienced great accomplishments. However, they were not fulfilled or satisfied because their accomplishments had nothing to do with their purpose. Saul was a good example of someone who did not understand his purpose. He spent many years trying to destroy the early Church through persecution. He was zealous and passionate about what he was doing, even though, what he was doing was not right. Saul, however, was ignorant as to what his purpose was. God knew what Saul's purpose was, and revealed it to him on the road to Damascus. This revelation transformed Saul (who was later named Paul), who having discovered his purpose, became a great missionary and apostle. This understanding led him to preach and teach with conviction, leading many to salvation.

Discovering and understanding your purpose will help you make good choices. Like Jesus, you must make sure that the choices you make please God. When you make it your business to know what the will of the Father is for you, then your choices should fall in line with His will.

Understanding your purpose causes you to produce fruit. When you become aware of your purpose in life, your joy will become 'full' and you will achieve at a high level. This is so because you are now focused. Your years of wondering who you are and what you should be doing are over. There's no more going around in circles or worrying about the uncertainty of where you may end up.

The exceptional person must know and understand her purpose. This understanding will make her life fruitful and free from frustrations and heartaches. Obedience in following the purpose given her by God will bring her promotion and victories.

CHAPTER TWO

Who do you see in the Mirror?

A mirror is very important if you want to get a good look at who you are. A mirror reflects the physical, outward appearance of oneself. A true authentic mirror is not deceptive or dishonest. It gives you the exact image of you. It also gives you a look at who you do not want to be. You can learn a lot from your mirror.

Much more important than the natural mirror is the spiritual mirror. To be an exceptional person, you must see yourself through a spiritual mirror. That spiritual mirror for the believer is the Bible, which is the infallible Word of God. You cannot go wrong when you use the Bible to guide you into becoming who you should be. We can easily be deceived by our minds into believing we are walking perfectly and producing spiritual fruit when our product is nothing more than superficial leaves. So often others are deceived by our external adornment and outward appearance. The real self is revealed through a spiritually objective observation.

Often we set up images of ourselves that do not reflect the real person. It takes a person with discernment to penetrate and see the deceptive images. An exceptional person is honest and transparent. He/she has no hidden agendas. Whatever one sees is who he/she is.

As was said before, the Bible is that special mirror. It reveals what our minds are inclined to when we are godly and when we are not. Godly persons are focused on obeying God and doing things that are pleasing unto Him. They are loving, caring and compassionate. They are not only concern about themselves, but seek always to take care of the needs and concerns of others. They do not mask who they are, but possess a genuine spirit and attitude.

We can also learn about ourselves by looking at others. Some people express themselves in ways that sometimes 'push our buttons.' Even though we may not recognize it initially, they can be major assets for us. Taking a closer look at them may reveal some things about us. Observing what we don't like in others helps us look deeper inside ourselves. We are challenged to look for similar traits and behaviors that need healing or changing.

Even though you may not like to think of persons who irritate you as mirror images of yourself, they are, and you can learn from them. Perhaps if you look hard and long enough, you may discover that the same angry, depressed, critical, or complaining person the mirror is reflecting, are the same traits that are operating in you. Often we feel that everyone except us have certain problems. But we only need to be honest with ourselves and start looking at the real us.

A mirror sometimes is magnified to give us a more enhanced look. In the same way, looking at ourselves through the reflection of someone else can make us feel like our situation is larger than life. Although you are not even close to being what seems to be reflected, seeing this behavior in your mirror will help you to address it before it gets out of hand. Sometimes we repress emotions and feelings so that we are not seen in a particular way. Often observing others can cause those dormant feelings to resurface in us

We do not have to go far to find mirrors. Our family, friends, and coworkers are all mirroring roles. They may not realize that they are helping us and we may not either. Our family members often play major roles of mirroring for us. They do this because it is more difficult for us to avoid and hide from them. Besides, running away and hiding from our mirrors is nonproductive. We feel that by avoiding someone who is reflecting us, our lives will be less stressful. However, that does not make us better. We need to stop avoiding our problems and address what is steering us in the face.

In order to be exceptional, it is vital that we change the way we think. When we have to deal with persons we find uncomfortable to be around, it is difficult to comprehend the grand opportunity to learn about ourselves. For us to move to that next level, we must shift our perspectives. As we make adjustments in our lives accordingly, our mirrors will reflect us differently. As we progress, we will always attract new mirror images.

Not only will we change, but will become mirrors for others. We should always be concerned about what others are learning through our actions each day. Be that exceptional person by reflecting positive attitudes every day.

CHAPTER THREE

Avoid Pitfalls

$\mathcal{E}$very person must understand that there is an enemy whose aim is to cause us to fail. After the fall of Satan, he turned his attention on mankind, creating havoc and mayhem. He has created pitfalls and traps to destroy us. It is important to recognize and avoid the plans and plots of the enemy. He is still using the same tactics he used on the angels who rebelled in heaven. Do not succumb to the adversary's temptations. Do not allow the spirits of disobedience and rebellion to overtake you.

One sure winning fight against the enemy is to renew your mind. Your success will be based on your thinking. Program your mind to receive and process only those things that will benefit you. Negative thinking will cause you to live a defeated life. The enemy's plan is to get us into doubt, fear, and faithlessness so that he can steal from us. He tries to control the way we think and behave so that the works of the flesh is produced in us. We must be positive thinkers if we are going to please God. He wants to get glory out of our lives.

The mind is that place that is often referred to as the battlefield. The battlefield is that area that the Holy Spirit and the enemy fight for control. They both compete for position and occupancy. The battlefield is that place where good and evil battle for the soul.

So many people fall into the trap of the enemy and for years live defeated lives. One way to overcome the snares of the enemy is to live in the Spirit. The Word of God instructs us to walk after the Spirit and not after the flesh. The flesh will keep us in bondage to the enemy.

As we are confronted by life's challenges, problems, issues, and decisions, we tend to become very impulsive. This impulse causes us to rush to resolutions without ever assessing the full consequences of our actions. We make decisions that are many times detrimental to us. After realizing our mistakes, we then try to validate our actions. We must remember to pray and seek answers from God for whatever we are facing. Always stay calm and take the time to think through every situation carefully. Look at the situation objectively and through a sound reasoning eye and then being led by the Spirit, come to a decision. Arriving at decisions and acting without taking just a moment to think, could lead to your downfall. Never act first before you think about what you want to do. Thinking first will cause you to avoid costly pitfalls and mistakes. Always weigh your options before your actions.

Many Christians are faced with temptations that are setup as pitfalls. It is important for them to understand that temptations or tests come in many forms, but the main reason is to destroy. Some things that could lead to pitfalls are:

- The cravings of the flesh (preoccupation with gratifying physical desires).
- The lusts of the eyes (preoccupation with material gain and beauty).
- The pride of life (boasting of what one has, does and can do) -preoccupation with status, importance and power.

Believers must fortify themselves against these temptations if they are going to avoid the ultimate downfall. God's power at work through His Holy Spirit, will insulate you from any temptation. Sometimes temptations are allowed to refine and strengthen us.

I often see godly people fall for sex and money. It seems in recent times that so many are having problems remaining faithful to the commands of God, especially where these are a concern. These are all pitfalls that are designed to embarrass us and even destroy us. The exceptional person must be one who is strong and can stand. He/she must learn to think with his/her brain and not with his/her emotions. I know that people are sometimes faced with numerous challenges. For some, finances are a major challenge, and they may even have to take on other jobs to survive. This challenge must be a major issue if you have children to care for. But these are times to trust God for help and strength, for provisions and favor. God is still faithful and cares about you and what you are experiencing. Know that He will never leave you nor forsake you. I know when you are going through hard times, it seems like your situation is bigger than life. Know that God is faithful and will never forsake you.

Regardless of the temptations and trials we are faced with during this time, we should always remember that God will help us. We have an example in Jesus who was tempted and tested in every way. (Hebrews 4:15; Matthew 4:1-11; Mark 1:12; Luke 4:1-13). He showed us that just as he overcame the temptations and was victorious, we have the power to do the same.

God will not allow us to be tempted beyond what we can bear (1 Corinthians 10:13). Whatever we are faced with, we can be assured that His power is available to help us. God will never forget us. In His Word, He made us the promise never to leave or forsake us. He will make a way of escape. Always be assured that His grace is sufficient, and our strength is made perfect in weakness.

You can achieve a better tomorrow if you avoid and learn from the mistakes made by others, and if you practice thinking before acting. It is always best to weigh your options before acting. Another pitfall that so many face is that of placing blame. Blaming others for mistakes that you have made will only cause your life to go downhill. No matter the size of our mistakes, each of us must take responsibility for our actions, be it big or small. Truly taking a self-inventory and addressing the real issues in your life before moving on will be beneficial. Being whole in every part of your life is important to God.

A pitfall that is prevalent among believers is that of complacency. In order to become an exceptional person, you must be a committed individual. It is so easy to fall through the cracks and accept a "whatever attitude" if you do not make a conscious effort to be committed. If you are experiencing success, think about all of the things that contributed to it. There must be a willingness to challenge oneself regularly and push to the next level. If you are going to make it into the realm of 'exceptional,' you cannot be complacent. Every day you have to make a conscious effort to push a little further and achieve a little more. Sometimes you may only be able to take baby steps, but baby steps are better than no steps at all. Do not allow the spirit of complacency to sabotage your forward and upward motion. Find success in life by deciding to make commitment a lifestyle.

Finally, make up your mind to always be a learner. So many have chosen to stop learning. Learning should be a lifestyle for the exceptional individual. It is easy to think that you have reached a certain level, and you do not need to go further. However, continuing to develop is important. Fresh ideas and new concepts are always in reach for grasp. There should always be a desire to embrace these ideas and concepts to help you become even more knowledgeable. Do not allow the pitfall of discontinuing learning to take a hold of you. Stay informed and be able to help others through your wealth of knowledge and resources. You are likely to be facing bigger and new challenges all of the time. So rather than needing less, you need more learning and development.

CHAPTER FOUR

God's Plan for You

*S*ometimes we find it difficult to determine God's will and plan for our lives. To avoid confusion and frustration, we must find a clear direction. We know from scriptures that our Father God knows everything about us. He knows our end from our beginning. He knows all that we are going to say and do and knows how long we will live. He is the Master Architect and does not want to leave anything to chance. If we go to Him in sincerity of heart, He will reveal a blueprint for our lives. He knows that no two persons are the same, but each is unique. He has a plan that is tailor-made just for you. He has given us all certain interests and desires, and then uses them to point us where He wants us to go.

If we want to find out God's plan for our lives, all we need to do is ask Him. Saul of Tarsus asked in Acts 9:6 "Lord what wilt thou have me to do?" Later he became Paul the

Apostle. Architects follow blueprints to construct buildings. Our Father has a blueprint for each of us as well.

God's plan for our lives is a practical one. He will not expect us to do what we are incapable of performing. He will give us the strength and wisdom to fulfill everything that He asks of us. Planning our lives outside the will of God leads to disaster.

God's plan for your life means that you will obey Him and do His will. He will reveal his plan for us step by step. Psalms 37: 23 says "The steps of a good man are ordered by the Lord, and he delighteth in his way." The Lord desires complete submission as He unfolds His plan. We must delight in the Lord and desire to obey Him. We need to recognize His voice and allow Him to lead us.

Prayer is one way through which God speaks to us. Spending quality time with God will reveal a step by step plan for your life. We need to take the time to seek God in prayer on a regular basis. We must find the time to get in His presence and listen to His voice. The more we spend time in prayer, the more familiar we become with God's voice and leading. We will sense and experience His leading in our lives as we yield ourselves to Him through prayer.

Another avenue through which God reveals Himself to us is His Word. There are times when we struggle for

God's guidance. The following scripture guides us as to which way God wants us to go: "Thy word is a lamp to my feet, and a light to my path." (Psalm 119:105) We can find guidance and solace in the Word of God. Let's use His Word to illumine our pathway. As we study and meditate upon His holy Scriptures, we will learn His will for our lives. Our success depends on knowing God's Word. As we spend time searching the scriptures, hidden truths will be revealed to us. These revelations can help to chart the course of our lives, thereby bringing success.

Circumstances or events are other ways by which we sense the leading of God. As you are seeking God's direction, events may establish what you have already felt God telling you to do. There are times when God will cause doors to open for you to walk through and find help for your present need. Then at other times, He will close doors to prevent us from impending failures or dangers. They don't just happen by chance! I believe that the reason a door has opened to us is that God wants us to go through it. The challenges in our lives often lead us to a place of pain and destruction. But at the end of it all, we discover that what we thought was ending in disaster turned into blessings. Remember, according to Jeremiah 29:11, his plans for us are good plans.

Many times when we are struggling with indecision, God uses other believers to help us find His plan for our lives. This plan may be revealed through someone on the radio, the singing of a song or the preaching of a sermon or even through one of our friends. A friend or coworker may encourage us without even knowing. However God chooses to communicate with us, we must be receptive. Having a relationship with God, will help us to discern that what we sense or feel is truly His plan for us. Perhaps it may take Him speaking through more than one person before we figure out that His plan for us is being confirmed. When we recognize the confirmation, then we will know it is time to step out in faith. Maybe we need to take that first step of faith and watch God confirm His plan for us as we go.

There are many scriptures laying out his plans for us. If we believe His Word, then we must believe that He has a plan for us.

PART TWO

Reprogram Your Mind

CHAPTER FIVE

Looking Through the Correct Lenses

*I*f we are going to see ourselves in the correct way, then we must look at ourselves through the eyes of God. Take a good look at yourself. What do you see? How do you view yourself? How do you feel about yourself? We cannot afford to base our self-worth on how others see us or on what we have accomplished. We sometimes characterize ourselves based on our feelings from the past and our looks. These things often cause us to set unrealistic goals and standards for ourselves.

We cannot live our lives the way others want us to, trying to get them to love us. We must have high self-esteem and feel secure in who we are. We should not give people permission to evaluate us based on our action; certainly we should not allow them the power to determine our self-worth.

Even after we become adults and are capable of making decisions, we sometimes internalize others instructing us on what to do. Can you identify with that? Perhaps you had a parent that criticized you often. Can you remember statements such as, "That's not responsible," or "Why are you doing it that way?" Some persons who may have had parents who were critical or verbally abusive allowed themselves to see themselves based on what their parents have told them.

Too often, many of us are so concerned that we are loved by others, that we give them permission to evaluate our self-worth. We may sacrifice our identity to get the attention and acceptance of the opposite sex, even to the extent of giving up our comfort. Some people try to lose weight to please others. They allow themselves to live by the opinions of those around them. They must understand that they are special. Being special is born out of the fact that we are children of God and joint-heirs with His Son Jesus Christ. We do not have to be manipulated and controlled by the standards of the world. We have a spiritual inheritance that is one of forgiveness and intimate relationship with Jesus Christ. We have a glorious and wonderful hope of spending all eternity enjoying fellowship with God. It is this knowledge that gives us comfort, peace, security and hope.

This truth is not based on the world's definition of identity, but on who we are in God, and who he has already made us.

1Peter 1:4 "To an inheritance incorruptible, and undefiled, and that fadeth not away, reserved in heaven for you,"

Sometimes we allow what has happened to us in the past to hold us captive and strangle and suffocate our forward mobility. You may be carrying a lot of shame and guilt. You may feel ashamed about certain aspects of the family you grew up in, or perhaps are embarrassed about sinful habits that you have struggled with for a long time. Maybe you have had an abortion or an affair in your past, and the weight of shame is almost unbearable. Perhaps something has been done to you, such as sexual assault, molestation, physical or emotional abuse. These are all painful and heart-wrenching situations that only God can heal. We have to surrender everything to him so that we can be free of them.

We do not have to continue struggling with issues from our past. If we do not release them, they will continue to control us in some way in our present and future. Thank God, they don't have to hold us hostage any longer. We can be free from past sin, embarrassing family histories, as well as past violations to our bodies and minds.

It is important to identify if what we are feeling in these situations is shame that can be destructive or guilt that is unhealthy. Guilt that is healthy will separate our identity from our behavior. Shame combines our guilt and behavior, so wrong actions make us have a negative image of ourselves. Healthy guilt makes us aware of the fact that we have done something that is in complete opposition to our values and moral standards.

When a believer does something wrong, the guilt that is experienced is a God-given emotion. It raises "red flags" that remind us that our behavior is an act of rebellion against God. It pushes us to acknowledge that we have done wrong, feel sorry for it, and then spurs us to confess our sin. This confession leads us to experience the love and forgiveness that God has provided for us through Jesus Christ.

After confessing our sin, we know longer have to carry guilt and shame. Although we still have to live with the consequences of sin, God does not destroy us for our sin. Through chastisement, He encourages us to move back on the right path. In this way, we can enjoy the full benefits of what He has for us. Often our struggles bring us closer to God, increasing our faith in Him and trusting Him to strengthen us when we are weak.

Are you overtaken by depression because of what you see when you look at yourself? Many persons struggle with depression at some point in their lifetime. Depression can be a biological one or one that is the result of a situation:

and often it can be the result of both. Often depression is caused by trying to live up to standards that are so high and seem unreachable. This constant striving for reaching a standard, can wear persons out, cause them to feel like failures and put them into a state of depression.

We have a way as women, of making the mistake of feeling responsible for not just themselves, but others as well. Being connected to family and friends, cause them to feel a sense of responsibility for them. We sometimes take on the weight and problems of everyone around us. Sometimes we find it difficult to separate who we are from what we do. We try to measure up to what we feel others expect us to. Often we wear ourselves out, trying to take care of the needs of those around us. We will burn ourselves out if we try to take care of everyone. This can eventually put a strain on us that leads to a whirlwind of stress and pain.

We have to become aware of what we are doing to ourselves and work at changing the way we do things. This is the right time to rely on the grace of God. His grace is available to us if only we humble ourselves to accept it. God's grace is his gift to us when we need strength and healing, and brings us freedom to live a new life. We cannot fix everyone and their problems. Each must be responsible for seeking their solutions, even though we may be able to help sometimes.

Once we embrace the gift of grace offered us by God our Father, we will be able to reach out and extend grace to those around us. We will line up our thinking with the way God views us; then we will refuse to live up to the distorted beliefs that the world has in place. Our attention will be turned away from what is going on with us, and we will have a greater desire to help others. If you are going to thrive and become the exceptional person that you are meant to become, you must remove the barriers that stand in your way. It is vital that you identify which barriers affect you most. Find a quiet place alone so that you can think about your life. Be objective! Look for new ways to look at yourself and ensure that your thought patterns are positive ones that would be more beneficial to you. Whenever you are faced with negative thoughts our behavior, take authority over them, cast them down and push them out of your mind. Always replace negative thoughts and behavior with the positive. It is important to renew your mind every day. Align your view with that of God. Before we give our lives to the Lord, our real sense of who we are is skewed. However, when we become born again, we receive the change that we so desperately need. We now have a new perception of ourselves and can see ourselves as God sees us. When we are operating in the world's system, our minds are cluttered with thoughts that could only take us downward. In that system, we subject ourselves to its operations and filter everything through its negative grid system.

For survival, we must make a decision to choose the right path. We cannot continue believing the lies the have been set out for us to believe. We must begin believing the truth. It may be difficult and feel uncomfortable at first, but believing the truth is a freeing experience. We must not adjust to the world's belief system.

God laid out a wonderful plan that shows and tells us who we are. We have to cooperate with that plan in order for us to be successful.

Unless we learn to look at ourselves like God looks at us, we'll never reach the potential that He has for us. Often the enemy bombards our mind and comes against our thoughts about who we are. He tries to condemn us and make us doubt ourselves. However, we can protect our minds by declaring the Word of God to ourselves. Our mental pictures of ourselves should be changed not according to some worldly view, but to how God sees us. We cannot even allow things that may have happened in the past hold us hostage. We need to realize that we are not who we used to be. We have been made new.

Where would we be now had Jesus felt like He did not measure up to what God had for Him? What if He felt too unworthy to take on the sins of the whole wide world? Wow! What state would we be in today?

We must learn to agree with God. We don't know everything, but God does. He sees the past, present and future! We are His workmanship. He is the Potter, and we are the clay in His hands. We must let Him work with us to continue to mold and shape our lives into what He sees is best. He knows the plans He has for us. The way God thinks about us should cause us excitement. Would you not consult the manual of a new item to ensure that you are using it properly? We should also look to God's Word (the blueprint or manual) so that our lives are patterned and fashioned correctly.

How do you see yourself? Whose eyes do you see yourself through? Are you viewing yourself through the eyes of your family or friends? Do you value their opinion of you more than God's opinion? Do you label yourself and determine who you are based on the negative opinions of others? Are you speaking negatively about yourself because of the way you view yourself? Do statements like this come out of your mouth? "I will never get ahead in life." I encourage you to stop putting down what God has lifted up. You can accomplish anything you want to through Christ Jesus.

You are so much better than how you are viewing yourself. In God's eyes, you are special. You are more than you think you are and have everything within you to succeed and be great. Yes! If you change the way you look at yourself, you will see how wonderful you are. Do not doubt yourself and allow failure to work in your life. Do not allow your thinking and speaking to condemn you and hinder your upward mobility. Practice speaking positively to yourself.

You may not feel worthy of God's grace because of things that happened in your past. But you are worthy because God says you are. You are worthy to receive and embrace ALL that He has given you. It's not about your feelings, but it's all about your faith. When we live by faith, we please God. It is your time to look and move ahead. Take hold of everything God has for you. Come on! Take a closer look at yourself! You are indeed EXCEPTIONAL.

CHAPTER SIX

Change Your Thinking and Develop a New Mindset

*H*ow we perceive ourselves, determines our behavior. If we think we are inadequate, we act that way. If we think we are beautiful, then that is how we will behave.

The journey towards happiness and authenticity is not determined by something outside us, but rather by our thinking, our thought process and our perception of who we are.

So if our way forward feels stagnant, we may want to look at the way we perceive ourselves. It could be that we are allowing fear and uncertainty to dominate us and rob us of the confidence that we need to move forward. Many times, we allow our forward motion to be affected by the past. Those unhealed hurts and pain may be causing us to skew our perceptions and recreate the same situations over and over.

The way we see a situation determines a different reaction and each reaction creates a different outcome. The way we perceive ourselves can 'make us or break us.' Negative perceptions can lead us down a road of destruction and allow great opportunities to pass us. Positive perceptions can take us to incredible new possibilities. It is important that we see ourselves the way God sees us. If we perceive ourselves as being victims, then the possibility exists for us to allow ourselves to be victimized.

Do not allow the thought of failing cause you not to try. Don't see the wall as a barrier preventing your forward motion, but instead take the challenge, muster up the strength and climb over it up knock it down. No matter what situation with which you are faced, use it as an opportunity to show that you are a conqueror and an overcomer.

We must use every opportunity to advance in life.

Don't see the wall as a barrier preventing your forward motion. Instead, take the challenge, muster up the strength, climb over it or knock it down. No matter the situation with which you are faced, use it as an opportunity to show that you are a conqueror and an overcomer. Remember, that all things are possible with God's help. Allow Him to help you renew your mind, your thought processes and thinking. The Word of God admonishes us to be transformed by the renewing of our minds. Changing our perception does not happen overnight. It is a process where we must move forward a little every day. We must avail ourselves to the Holy Spirit so that He can bring about the changes in us. Despite what is happening in our lives, God's Holy Spirit can change our situation. In order to improve our situation, it starts with changing the way we think.

We have to make the decision to think different. We have to choose to see ourselves the way God sees us, and change the way we think. We have to remember that God does not see things the way that we see them. We cannot allow negative thoughts to control us. It is important that we dispel negative thoughts from our minds. Do not believe the bad reports from the enemy. God's promises are sure. He will never leave or forget about us. He wants the best for us and promises to work all things for our good. His plans for our lives are good, and our future in Him is secured if we trust Him.

Our thoughts are related to who we are, and who we will become. Right now, we all believe things about ourselves. Some of those things may be true, and some may be false. Whatever those things are, they become a part of who we are if we continue to focus on them. It is possible for us to become eventually whatever we are thinking about the most.

If the enemy can take hold of our mind, it can become a stronghold to us. Therefore, we must fight for control of our thought life. Renewing our minds means learning to recognize what thoughts are from God, and what thoughts are from the enemy, and then conditioning our minds with those thoughts that are godly. We must pattern our thoughts after God's Word. Even though all sorts of thoughts may popup in our minds, we have the right to choose which ones we will erase and the ones we will keep. The mind is the battleground of the Holy Spirit and the enemy. The Holy Spirit should always be victorious in having that control over our minds. We need a renewed mind in order to carry out Kingdom agendas. What we believe about ourselves will determine our response to Satan.

CHAPTER SEVEN

Be a Person of Integrity

*P*ersons who are scrupulous and dishonest will never get ahead. Living with integrity is so much easier than living a life of deceit. Banishing integrity for a life of deceit and dishonest behavior will always eventually take its toll. A person who chooses a life of lies and deceit, hide and misrepresent the truth. True happiness will never be had by deceitful people. They will always have a struggle trying to remember the lies they told. They will always have a fear of getting caught one day. This is not the life for anyone to live. It is better to be a person of integrity. Living with integrity brings comfort, peace and wholeness. When your conscience is pure, you can rest easy knowing that you have done what is right.

A person of integrity is reliable and dependable. Others know that if that person promises something, he will deliver on his or her promise. This is the kind of person who would be given greater responsibility on the job because he can be trusted. Proverbs 31 talks about the virtuous woman. This woman was trustworthy and honest. Verse 11 says, "The heart of her husband doth safely trust in her, so that he shall have no need of spoil." It is so important that you live in a way that others can place their confidence and trust in you. When you are entrusted with confidential information, lock those secrets away. Nothing erodes a friendship faster than a breach of trust. Your family and friends should be able to confide in you, knowing that their information is secured. When you live a life of integrity, all of your relationships will be healthier, stronger, and more satisfying.

Integrity is a character that should be developed and practiced. It should become a lifestyle; not something that is done one day and ignored the other. Living a life of integrity is a daily process that should be a part of you for the rest of your life. So many people compromise their integrity. It is vital that you make a decision now on what kind of person you are going to be. You have a responsibility of choosing to be a person of good moral standards. Choosing to be this kind of person puts you in a position to make the right choices when in the midst of crisis or is faced with temptations. If you do not decide beforehand, you may take the easy way out when faced with pressure in a situation. The easy way could lead you down a path of disaster and pain. Don't compromise on the little things, and you won't on the bigger ones. Decide now what you will and will not compromise on. This way, when faced with tough choices, you would have already decided what you will do. Nothing is more valuable than your good name and the ability to see yourself each day with a clear conscience. No one else can take responsibility for your life. You have to take personal responsibility for your decisions and actions. A person of integrity takes responsibility for both their successes and failures. It is easy to try to blame others for your failures and mistakes. People of integrity own up to their mistakes and take responsibility for their shortcomings. They also never shy away from apologizing, but make it a point to do so when necessary.

While a person of integrity should be honest with others, the first step is being honest with himself. Be true to yourself and who you are. Say what you mean and mean what you say at all times. Always be true to your word.

Let integrity be seen in every area of your life. If you are an employee, then integrity should be seen in your work. Do the job that you were hired to do with excellence. Don't expect to be paid for work that you did not do and time you did not work.

Be a person of integrity even in your relationships. Be transparent in everything you do and never leave room for there to be questions. If you are married, don't keep secrets from your spouse. Be an open book. Hiding valuable information from your spouse or being dishonest will erode the trust between you. Always, follow-through with the things you promised to do. "A man's word is his bond." If you are unable to do what you have promised, don't act like it's no big deal. Talk to your spouse and explain why you cannot do it as promised.

PART THREE

Change Your Way of Speaking

CHAPTER EIGHT

Words are Powerful

$\mathcal{H}$ave Your Words Ever Gotten You Into Trouble? Words are more powerful than you realize. They have the power to wound or heal, discourage or encourage, tear down or build up. Do you ever think about the words you speak and the power they carry? I challenge you to monitor your words for a day: notice whether they're positive or negative and notice the effect they have. Don't only focus on the words you speak to other people. Take notice of the words you speak to yourself as well. Pay close attention to see what words you habitually say to yourself. What do you tell yourself about yourself?

Perhaps you'll be surprised at how many negative things you say. It's time to stop and think about the words you speak and the effect they have on you and other people. It's time to speak words that will change your life and help to transform the lives of the people around you. Remember, "Death and life are in the power of your tongue."

Words can have emotional, physical and spiritual impact. The words you speak can edify or discourage. They can build someone up or dampen their spirit. The words that you speak are so powerful. They can cause physical changes in your body; they can change the atmosphere in a room; they can make someone smile or make them cry.

You are created in God's image. Like God, you have the power to make things happen with your words. Your words have more power than you may imagine. There's something creative and powerful about the words you speak. That's why you need to think before you speak.

Did you know that the words you speak can be a powerful weapon of destruction or a mighty instrument of peace? The words you speak are so amazingly powerful that they can inject death or life into a situation. You must become conscious of what you are saying so that you can choose to exercise self-control. The words that you speak can bring life or death to you and others. It's time to think before you speak. If after weighing your words, you determine that the words you are about to speak are kind, true, necessary and helpful, then say it as lovingly and gentle as you can. Remember, once the words go forth, you can never bring them back!

Have you ever heard the expression: "Sticks and stones may break my bones, but words will never hurt me?" Words will not break your bones or hurt you in a physical way, but they can harm and hurt a person in other ways. Even the strongest, confident person can be affected by negative words. Negative words can lead to you doubting yourself and displaying negative behaviors. Negative words can also lead to you hurting someone's feelings. Many times we may not realize how harsh our words can be to someone, even when what we are saying is true. Harsh words can create rifts and destroy relationships that may never be mended. Proverbs 15:1 says, "A soft answer turneth away wrath: but grievous words stir up anger." We must be careful with how we use our tongues and what we allow to come out of our mouths.

The words we speak and hear can shape our lives. Words have the power to heal or to hurt. It is very important for us to become aware of how and what we are speaking. You do not have to struggle with negative thoughts and feelings because of the words that you are speaking or hearing. Positive speaking and affirmations are great ways to reprogram oneself. To ensure the effectiveness of the affirmations, focus your energy on your heart and repeat them with attention and conviction. Always have a strong desire to have God's best by speaking positive words into your life. If you are used to negative speaking and you've made a mistake as you try to change, counteract those negative words with positive ones.

"Pleasant words are as an honeycomb, sweet to the soul, and health to the bones". Proverbs 16:24

Have you ever been on the receiving end of someone who has unleashed their mouth on you one day, spewing out words full of hatred or criticism? I am sure that it felt like darts being shot through your heart. Like a warrior sharpens the head of an arrow, I can only imagine how that person must have carefully sharpened his/her words that he/she was going to launch at you. Then, perhaps at your most weakest and vulnerable moment they aimed and carefully launched their weapon of attack right at your heart. If your heart were not guarded when they attack, those words could penetrate deep, sometimes wounding you for years. When you think about how a negative attack made you feel, you should never want to be the one to release negative words. You should want to treat others the way that you wish to be treated.

Our words can bring life to a situation if we speak them properly. A word of encouragement spoken at just the right time to someone who is discouraged can release life to that person. Maybe you had been the recipient of that word of life just when you needed it. There are so many people who are in a pit of despair and feel like giving up. Perhaps all they need is for someone to show them love or appreciation. Maybe they just need a pat on the back and words like "thank you for what you are doing." You will be amazed to know how those kind words could lift someone's spirit and pull them back onto the right path.

The words that come out of our mouths originate in the heart. Jesus makes a direct connection between our hearts and our mouths in the scripture verse below.

"O generation of vipers, how can ye, being evil, speak good things? for out of the abundance of the heart the mouth speaketh." Matthew 12:34

In the two scriptures below, Jesus gives us clear understanding as to how we should use our words. It is obvious that we will be held accountable for the words that we speak.

"But I say unto you, that every idle word that men shall speak, they shall give account thereof in the day of judgment." Matthew 12:36

"For by thy words thou shalt be justified, and by thy words thou shalt be condemned." Matthew 12:37

Again, our words are powerful, and we must be careful what we do with them. Choose to declare words that will advance yourself and others. Choose to speak words that will do the following:

1. Give life
2. Uplift
3. Encourage
4. Express love and compassion
5. Heal

Refuse to use words that will:

1. Cause death
2. Tear down and destroy
3. Discourage
4. Cause hurt and pain
5. Cause harm

I am always careful of persons who love to engage in gossip and idle talking. Gossip is a terrible weapon of destruction. Gossipers love to reveal personal information about others. They love to involve themselves in the business of others. Most times they create a whole lot of confusion, discord and pain. There are many things that we are told or know about that are not meant to be repeated. Repeating them would only lead to hurt and harm. Have you ever heard someone say to you, "Don't tell anyone that I said this?" If it is not worth repeating then perhaps it was not worth saying in the first place! When spreading gossip, sometimes the gossiper pretends that it is with great reluctance that he/she speaks and that he/she is "very grieved to even repeat what's being said. However, if he/she was grieved, then he/she would not have said anything.

The best way to destroy gossip is to refuse to be a willing participant. Gossip will not survive if you decide not to listen to it or engage in the conversation. Gossip is prevalent because too many people enjoy hearing and eagerly engaging in the latest rumor. They are just as guilty as the one who gossips. If you express disdain for gossiping and evil talking, the person who loves to gossip will not return to you.

There are many examples in the Word of God that points to gaining good results through positive speaking. Positive speaking and thinking will bring about great changes in your life, leading to positive results. Thinking and speaking positively can bring healing, prosperity and joy to an individual. Speak with confidence, believing that what you say will happen because it is the will of God. Correct speaking will cause the power of God to create a life changing atmosphere for you. When you release words that are filled with love, they bring blessings to us and others. Words of wisdom can encourage and uplift our spirits and bring healing and restoration to our bodies and souls. How you speak about yourself and others has a direct bearing on the mind. We have the ability to create or environment and situation simply by what we declare. Our words should be filled with faith and love. What we say makes a vast difference in our lives. Our words are the keys to abundant life. Unlock the door to your life of abundance by keeping a watch on what you say.

CHAPTER NINE

Annihilate Negative Words Spoken Against You

At times in our lives, we face obstacles that seem overwhelming! Those obstacles can come from persons around us speaking negative words and having negative attitudes. Often we listen to them and allow them to penetrate and resonate in our spirits. These actions sometimes lead to a downward spiral. Not everyone will support our decisions and choices or help make our lives more accomplished and successful. Not everyone is happy when we are succeeding in life or are being blessed. We cannot afford to allow negative people and their negative words to cause our downfall. We have to focus on the goals before us if we are going to achieve anything. Never allow others to derail you from accomplishing the things that are before you.

You have the power to annihilate every negative word spoken against you. Those thoughts and imaginations can come in the form of others words and opinions. You have to believe that you have the power to cast down negative words launched against you and your forward motion.

In order to overcome negative words, you must first have confidence in what you are persevering to accomplish. Never be in a position of uncertainty about who you are and what you are doing. Although the path may be one that takes some work and effort on your part, be vigilant and do the work. Always connect with persons who will give positive advice and offer sound judgment. Refuse the advice of persons offering advice that is filled with doubt and unbelief. Even though we may not have full understanding of all that we are trying to accomplish, there are people that can help us create the methods and procedures to accomplish them. We need the help of us because we do not know and understand everything. So we must possess the ability to listen and take instructions from those who have a proven method even if we do not understand all that they are saying. We also through prayer can ask our heavenly Father to enlighten our understanding and give us the wisdom and knowledge that we need.

In order to discern and decipher what is best for us, we must understand who we are. We will have no need of wondering which words to accept and which to pull down.

As believers, we must not be ignorant of Satan's devices. He is cunning and crafty and will trick us into accepting things that are bad for us. How often do we see people put their trust in persons they believed had their backs, only to be left disappointed and even confused. Not everyone who looks like they want your best does.

Curses and negative words come in various forms. They are not all of the death threat variety or even obvious. Many of them are very subtle and deceptive. Negative words can be spoken to you by well-meaning people in your life. You can even curse yourself by constantly speaking about your problems, fears and worries. For you, these may be harmless, innocent acts, but they can have a huge effect on your life. Any negative word spoken by someone or yourself can turn into a curse. One good example is listening to a repetitive media report about a deadly disease. This repetition can instill fear in you and the negative words can influence you to believe the worse. This may lead to constantly speaking about it, which in turn reinforces the fear in your mind. This reinforcement can subsequently cause you fear of having the disease as well. Fear and negative information can seriously affect your emotions. Being sad, angry, or stressed can suppress your immune system that over time can lead to all kinds of health issues.

You may ask, "How do I pull down curses and annihilate negative words spoken against me?" Well, the power is in your tongue. Just as words can produce harm, they can also produce good. Make it a lifestyle to decree and declare words over your life that will release blessings and pull down negative words and curses. You may not even know what has been spoken against you, but you can pray in ways that will destroy those unknowing words anyhow. Job 22:28 declares, "Thou shalt also decree a thing, and it shall be established unto thee: and the light shall shine upon thy ways."

The curses and negative words spoken against us may seem innocuous and harmless at the time, but they can be very destructive if not dealt with. Just as positive words can build up, comfort and encourage, leading to life, negative words can tear down, discourage and destroy, leading to death. James 3:6 says "And the tongue is a fire, a world of iniquity: so is the tongue among our members, that it defileth the whole body, and setteth on fire the course of nature; and it is set on fire of hell."

It is so important that we guard our tongue. Proverbs 21:23 says "Whoso keepeth his mouth and his tongue keepeth his soul from troubles." Our words carry enormous weight and affect us and others more than we sometimes think. They often impact our lives for decades for good or bad. Ephesians 4:29 says "Let no corrupt communication proceed out of your mouth, but that which is good to the use of edifying, that it may minister grace unto the hearers."

Pleasant and positive words spoken can bring edification and healing to the hearer. Wholesome words build up and empower people. Unpleasant and corrupt words spoken can discourage and diminish someone, even causing hurt and damage. We should always extend grace through the words that we speak.

CHAPTER TEN

Destroy Mediocrity and Complacency

A person who does not perform well at anything is considered a mediocre person. I believe that "mediocrity" is a spirit. We were not created to be average or moderate. We were not created to accept a life of complacency and remain in a state of stagnancy. We have the ability to be exceptional, always flowing at our optimum. The spirit of excellence should always be seen in everything we do and say. The potential is in us to achieve highly. If you are operating in the spirit of mediocrity and complacency, are you ready to get rid of them and unleash your greatness? If you are, then keep on reading to discover how you can get rid of mediocrity and step into a life of remarkable.

Mediocrity is responsible for causing many people fail in achieving their goals and dreams. They have no clue as to how to tap into their full potential and move into a life of greatness. First there must be an understanding that greatness is inside of you. You have the ability to do so much more than you probably think you can.

Many people do not try because they do not want to make the steps necessary to get to where they should. Often they procrastinate because they are focusing on the process rather than the reward. In order to achieve greatness, you may have to do some things that are not comfortable. For example, you may be overweight and want to lose those extra pounds. Those unwanted pounds will not fall off by you just simply thinking about it or wanting them too. You have to put effort and work into making it happen. You will also have to give yourself time to go through the process necessary to get the weight off. If will not happen overnight. Think about it, if you have to wake up early in the morning to go to a gym, and you focus on the process rather than the reward, you may never do it. However, if you focus on the reward you will get after putting in the work, you may become highly motivated.

Improve the quality of your life by refusing to be mediocre. You have to understand that success is not something that is easily achieved. You will need to commit to whatever is required, take whatever action is needed and venture out of your comfort zone into places that may most likely be unfamiliar and even uncomfortable. You may have to do some things that you may not like doing in order to move into a place of greater. Unless you form a habit of doing certain things that you hate doing, you will never be successful.

Mediocre people live their lives based on feelings and emotions. They do not launch out into the deep to achieve the "more" that can be grasped. They stay near the shore, only to experience frustration. They do not put time into planning and forecasting. They do not set goals for their future. They live life on the edge.

Successful people set short and long term goals and work hard to achieve them. They put in the time necessary to make their dreams and aspirations reality. They take more risks and venture out of their comfort zones. They put in more effort and time than the average person and focus on the reward. This is what we all must to do if we are going to destroy mediocrity and complacency.

Planning is an absolute must if you are going to be successful. Whatever you have to do, make your plans before the day you are going to do it. Make it a habit to write down or record what you need to do ahead of time. Doing this will make it easier to meet your goals. You will be able to focus better, be more organized and more productive. You will better focus on what you will have to do on the next day.

If you are going to beat mediocrity, find out exactly what you want to accomplish in your life. Guessing will only keep you frustrated. You cannot afford to go through life trying your hands at anything, not being certain of what you want to do. If you do not know what you want to accomplish, you will never be able to tap into your greatness and achieve great results. You must clearly know what you want to achieve, so you reach your full potential.

Once you know for sure what you want to achieve, put some solid plans in place as to how you are going to achieve your goals. Many people just talk about what they want in their lives, but they never put a solid plan in place to achieve it. You cannot build your dream house if you do not have any vision of how it looks. You cannot build your dream house if you do not have plans drawn of how it should look and what it should be. You need to have a plan to achieve you goals. If you fail to plan, you will certainly plan to fail.

Come on! Get up from that seat of complacency and create a plan for your success. Create awesome results by taking great action. Don't just say you want to be debt-free, take some steps and put some actions in place that will lead you into a debt-free life. Wasting time only talking about your dreams, will not make them come true. You must act. Commit to working hard until you get the results you want. Being committed is how successful people produce amazing results in their lives. Make sure you have the willingness to keep on learning and improving. These are keys that will keep you on your journey to success. By constantly learning and improving, you will be able to achieve the results you want in a faster manner. When trying to get success, it is important to read, attend seminars and workshops and even enroll in courses related to what you are doing.

You should never be satisfied with just getting by with the minimum. Mediocrity stifles you, causing you to remain at the bottom or the back. We can only be successful if we change our behavior of performing at a mediocre level in all areas of our lives. It is only when we give our best will we appreciate our achievements and enjoy the benefits they bring.

Success in life depends on you being discipline. It is important that you approach every project with motivation and enthusiasm. Motivation will help you continue the journey that you have started. So often, people start out with the best of intentions, but because of the lack of motivation and drive, they fall off the 'band wagon.' So often, we give up too easily. As soon as the journey becomes arduous, we surrender to the pressure, cave in and give up. All it takes most times is that little extra push to get us to the place of earning the prize and achieving our goals and dreams.

Successful people gain their success using strategies. Putting strategies in place puts us in a safe position when trying to succeed. Strategies help us to banish mediocrity and develop stickability. Stickability distinguishes the successful from the unsuccessful.

Successful people are also flexible in the event the unexpected arises. You will be faced with obstacles at times. But being flexible and willing to break through barriers will help to destroy mediocrity or at least keep it at bay.

Remember, when you are trying to stamp mediocrity and complacency out of your life, you must give nothing less than your best. Regardless of how surmountable the task is, put your all into it and see it through successfully. Don't be so afraid of hard work that you always choose the safe and easy way out. It speaks to laziness, fear and yes, mediocrity. Always check to see if there is room for improvement and make adjustments where needed. When you know for sure where you are headed, do not be distracted by the crowd. Unless the crowd is headed in the same direction as you, do not follow it. Ignore them and remain focused. Unfortunately, many of us find ourselves trapped by the grip of mediocrity because we are afraid to be different. You do not have to be petrified of standing up and being true to yourself if you have a clear understanding of what you are doing. When you set the expectations for your success, you do not have to submit to the expectations of others. Do not miss out on the opportunity to live a better, more fulfilling and successful life because of what other people say? Don't be bound by other people's opinions and do not allow their dictates to influence you. Be so convicted by what you want that no one can take you off course. Move into to a life of excellence and success by choosing to get rid of mediocrity and complacency.

PART FOUR

Start Looking Ahead

CHAPTER ELEVEN

Bid the Past Goodbye

*W*e all go through life remembering or even holding onto certain negative feelings that are connected to situations that took place in the past. How we deal with these feelings differs from person to person. They are based on how we think, how we were raised and learned patterns of behavior. Holding on to the past and all the negative things that may have happened, is certainly not good for us.

Many people are held hostage by their past. Past mistakes and failures so often take a grip of the thoughts and actions of persons causing them to make wrong choices. It is vital that you confront the challenges of the past and make a resolve to leave them behind. A past left unresolved will continue to haunt you as you journey in life. If you do not address your past, it can hinder your way forward. Depending on what happened in the past, you may end up being faced with more sorrow, pain and anger. You may not want to revisit certain aspects of what happened in the past, but it is important to do so and resolve it.

If you allow yourself to become victim to the past, it can rob you of a wonderful future. It may not always be easy to do this by yourself. You may have to get help to guide you through it all.

Accept that you cannot change what happened. What has happened is in the past. It is not possible to rewrite the facts of what you experienced. However, it is possible to rewrite the way you perceive it and handle it from now onward. If you don't, your hurt could be carried over into new experiences and relationships, possibly being even worse than before.

Negative thoughts from the past usually surface when we are faced with similar situations. This is when positive thinking and letting go can help. Carrying all your past pain and sadness around with you will only hold you back in life. If you keep all those negative emotions inside you, then someday they would all come spilling out in a serious breakdown, no longer being kept locked under your control.

So we all need some way of letting go of these negative thoughts and feelings. The best way is to deal with them right away, soon after the event took place. Otherwise, you can keep dwelling on past pains and end up becoming a victim of these negative circumstances that have long since finished. So many people carry past hurts for many years, refusing to release them. Holding on to your hurts from the past, will only lead to further hurts and even physical illnesses. Why waste your precious time and energy on old stuff that cannot benefit you or help your future? No matter how much we bring things from the past into the present, no one can change what has happened in the past. If we continue to hold on to these negative events, they can become fears, taking over our lives, and clouding our decisions and good judgment. We must rid ourselves of bitterness and unforgiveness so that we can enjoy a rich future.

Once you are sure that you have addressed past hurts and failures, remove the past from your future. This simply means that you must learn to not allow past experiences to control and dominate your future relationships and aspirations. Refuse to take your past into your future. Accept that while you cannot change the past, you can cease to let it replay every time a new challenge arises.

Overcome past negative behaviors and wrong habitual reactions that can transfer into your present and future. Even if your past were heavily burdened with the worst, you could overcome. Be proactive and decide before hand what your actions will be if a situation arises. Your past has no right to control you. You have the authority to choose to cut the past loose. I know this may not be easy, but it is not impossible. It's the only way to enjoy life, without it being clouded and tainted with the problems of the past. You may have to take baby steps, but they are better than no steps at all. Each step brings you closer to achieving your goal. If you have to take it slowly, by all means do so. No overnight transformation will occur when you are trying to move yourself through past habits or hurts. It all takes time and if you are willing, you will only achieve the best results. You can greatly benefit from allowing yourself the time and space to move on. So start small, clear your mind of all past negative thoughts and start on your journey, right now.

Don't let negative thoughts or emotions stop you from being happy. Bid the past goodbye and look ahead to a new and exciting life. Create a great future for yourself. A great future begins when you are healed from past hurts, and you are strong, whole and healthy emotionally. This wholeness will allow you to be able to cope with and handle any negative scenarios that may come your way. If you want to have a glorious future, the power lies within you to create it. Learn to embrace the reality that your future can be as wonderful as you want it to be.

CHAPTER TWELVE

Get Rid of Fear

*M*any people struggle to conquer or even face their fears. For some, conquering fear takes nearly an entire lifetime, while others simply fail to deal with their fears at all. Fear is a gripping, crippling emotion that can hold its prey hostage for a very long time. It often limits the actions of an individual, as fearful people avoid things or situations that remind them of their fears. Unfortunately, everyone has his/her set of fears. How each individual chooses to deal with fear, determines the end result. The question is, will you control your fear or will you let it control you?

Fear is an emotional response to a perceived danger. People can acquire fears from painful incidents, bad memories, frequently heard stories, etc. Sometimes people can become completely intimidated by their fears, which may trigger episodes of anxiety, depression, panic and even violence. Fear has a way of dominating the mind. It may be difficult for some people to conquer their fears, but it is not impossible. Through prayer, practice and a total renewal of your mind, you can master your fears and eventually get rid of them.

At some point in life, you have to face and confront your fear. Running away from it will not help. You may have to ask yourself questions like: What do I fear? Why do I fear these things? What can I do to conquer my fears? It is vital that you answer these questions if you are going to stop fear from overpowering you. You can state all of your reasons why your fears are currently controlling you.

Most fears are birth through death or loss, humiliation, failure and pain. Death is usually the most difficult to deal with. Most people have an innate fear of the unknown and the uncertainty of the afterlife. Believers, however, have no reason to fear death, if they clearly understand the Word of God concerning life after death. Living life the way God commands us to, puts us in the position not to fear death. Walking in obedience to God is 'key' to not having fear of death.

For some people, fear is exaggerated. Perhaps this fear was introduced during childhood. A child has a completely different perspective on what he/she has experienced than that of an adult. For a child, something that is small could seem huge and dreadful. This fear can carry into adulthood and continue throughout that person's life. In order to deal with fear, you have to pinpoint the physical, mental and emotional effects it is having on you. If you are going to move to that place of being exceptional, you must get rid of your fears. A good place to start is to find affirming scriptures such as the ones below and begin to declare them over your situation on a regular basis.

2Timothy 1:7 "For God hath not given us the spirit of fear; but of power, and of love, and of a sound mind."

Romans 8:15 "For ye have not received the spirit of bondage again to fear; but ye have received the Spirit of adoption, whereby we cry, Abba, Father."

Isaiah 41:10 "Fear thou not; for I am with thee: be not dismayed; for I am thy God: I will strengthen thee; yea, I will help thee; yea, I will uphold thee with the right hand of my righteousness."

It is helpful to saturate your heart and mind with scriptures that will encourage you as you fight fear. It is alright to recite them silently to yourself, but it is so much more powerful when you speak them loudly into the atmosphere. Let the enemy know you mean business and that you don't intend to be bound by fear anymore. Coming to an agreement with what God says about you and declaring that into the atmosphere, brings change to your life.

Fear is an emotion and not necessarily a reality. We innately have the ability to respond quickly to danger. Sometimes we can feel that a situation is going to be scary before knowing that it is. We can set ourselves up to fear and react to something that is not real at all. We must avoid allowing negative scenarios to build in our mind. So often people take a fear and sketch out circumstances in their mind of what could happen. Very often, these scenarios are irrational. When faced with the emotion of fear, we must analyze its rationality. If it is based strictly on emotion and not reality, we should not even entertain it and dismiss it quickly. We cannot allow fear to dominate our lives and steal our joy. Perhaps the greatest secret to overcoming fear is walking in love. As we grow in our love for God, we will be better able to live our lives with a confident assurance that God is in full control.

CHAPTER THIRTEEN

❧

Unclutter Your Spirit by Forgiving

*I*f you are going to be exceptional, learning to forgive is a must. What exactly is forgiveness? Forgiveness is being able to release yourself from the pain someone has caused you and also release the person who caused the pain. It is letting go of resentment and anger and refusing to harbor hard feelings toward the wrongdoer. People often express forgiveness verbally, but in their hearts they have not truly forgiven. They are saying one thing, but doing another. As long as you are unable to forgive, you hold yourself in bondage. You cannot be completely happy or free until you let go of your hurt and anger. Otherwise, it will fester inside of you, take root and consume you like a disease. Unforgiveness hinders our faith and keeps us bound. It is important to practice the art of forgiveness.

The same way you expect to be forgiven, you should also forgive.

For some, it may be difficult to forgive those who have hurt you. However, it is one of the most important things you can do for yourself. Forgiveness is perhaps more beneficial to the person giving it than for the person receiving it. It is a freeing experience when given. Forgiving someone who has hurt you can be difficult. Asking for forgiveness can be just as difficult, but it is very important. Harboring resentment, hurt and anger can affect you mentally, physically and spiritually. Emotions and resentments left unresolved, can affect a person's mental state, making it difficult to concentrate and perform daily tasks. Allowing your mind to be cluttered by unforgiveness, creates distractions. Negative feelings and emotions left unchecked can affect you in numerous ways. So often, unforgiveness can cause a breakdown in relationships. Physical health also can suffer as a result of holding on to negative emotions. Carrying around anger and resentment can result in many different ailments; such as headaches, fatigue, lethargy and even high blood pressure. Also, one's Spiritual development and progress may become stagnant when he/she refuses to forgive. Forgiveness can help you to heal on all levels.

The process of forgiveness may take time. A disagreement between two individuals may be forgiven quickly, but if the hurt is very deep, forgiveness may be a gradual process.

You may need time to work through the pain before you can get to the place of forgiveness. Committing yourself to prayer, meditation and even fasting can help you reach that place.

Being honest with oneself is very important when going through the process of healing hurts. You must acknowledge and accept your feelings rather than deny them. Whether you are the one forgiving or the person asking for forgiveness, always operate in honesty and sincerity. Not only do you need to forgive others, but there may be times when you need to ask for forgiveness as well. Also, there may be situations when the need arises for you forgive yourself. If you cannot forgive yourself, it will be difficult to forgive others. Forgiveness heals the spirit and sets your mind and heart free. It is a necessary component to living a healthy life.

Everyone is faced with a situation at some point in life where they will have to grapple with issues of forgiveness. Holding on to anger, hatred and negative emotions, can take a toll on our bodies. As said before, unforgiveness has destructive effects on our mind, body and spirit. The energy we use to store these emotions or release them against others, creates hormonal changes in our bodies which can be damaging to our health. Furthermore, relationships are seriously affected and many times destroyed when we allow negative emotions and behaviors to dominate our lives. It is vital that we get rid of these emotions as quickly as possible and forgive persons that caused us hurt.

What about those situations in our lives where we feel we can never forgive? These are precisely the situations where we need most to practice the act of forgiveness. Practicing forgiveness protects us against being a victim twice over. Having a willingness to forgive, releases you from the powerful grip of being a victim. Forgiveness certainly frees us. It allows us to break the bonds of anger, rage, hatred, and vengeance. These are like toxins to our lives, leading us down the path of destruction. They prevent us from developing into the mature person we are supposed to be.

When forgiveness takes place, we naturally release the disturbing thoughts and emotions that drain our physical, mental, emotional and spiritual well-being. When we forgive, we enjoy the endless benefits that forgiveness brings. The result is better health, a greater level of joy and happiness and overall fulfillment. Forgiveness can release us from the past and put us on the road to great success. While giving forgiveness may not always be easy, it is certainly worth it. Unclutter your spirit by giving yourself and others the gift of forgiveness.

PART FIVE

Create a Happy and Fulfilled Life

CHAPTER FOURTEEN

Life is What You Make It

*L*ife for an individual is all about what he/she makes it. Often I hear the statement, "You are what you eat!" In the same way, what you put into life is what you will get out of it. When my children were younger, sometimes they would ask me to buy them something. At times, I have said to them that I did not have the money on me for what they wanted. Their response was always, "Well get it from the machine." By the "machine," they meant the "ATM." In their little minds, there was always money in the "machine," and all I had to do was push my card in and get it. They did not understand that in order to get money out of the machine, I had to make deposits to my account. Had I not made the deposits, I would not be able to retrieve any money from the "machine." What you deposit into your life, be it good or bad, will determine what you get out of it.

Everyone should want a good life. Enjoying a good life does not just happen. There are some necessary steps that one must take in order to have a life of fulfillment and happiness.

If you are going to move forward in life, you must first accept the reality of your situation for what it is. This will give you a clear picture of where you are and a point from which to start your move forward. In this way, you will be better able to determine the best direction to choose. To ignore this reality or to struggle against what is, will only be a waste of your time and energy. To remain in a stagnant position, wishing that things were different, or to pretend that they are, will prevent you from getting anywhere. Loosen your grip on the old and embrace the new. Do you hold on so tightly to what you are comfortable with, that you deny yourself the opportunity to learn and experience great new things? You can discover and enjoy a lot more if you are willing to let go of the fear of change. Let go and move into a place of accomplishments and happiness.

Your way forward is to look beyond what you can see, visualize the possibilities and chart a course ahead. Then take the challenge and make steps that will take you in the direction of your vision. If you are going to experience a wonderful, successful life, you must plan.

Planning provides us with the direction in which we should head. It gives us a clear picture of what we need to do and how to get to where we want to go. It strengthens our confidence in understanding what measures are best to achieve the goals ahead. Planning also helps us to analyze alternative courses of action that we should take. It enables us to examine our path carefully and makes us aware of possible pitfalls and their likely consequences.

When we plan for our lives, we significantly reduce uncertainties. There are always things hidden to us that we may not see upfront. It forces us to make changes that are necessary for our continuous success. Persons who do not plan, run the risk of having to make impulsive decisions. Planning takes the guesswork out of the equation, making for a smoother transition. It reduces the probability of major errors and even failures along the way.

The world is filled with resources that can assist you in making your life better. Those resources are available to you in abundance. It is up to you to reach for as many of them as you need and use them to your advantage. Adopt the attitude that you are not owed anything, and if you are going to get something from life, you must work hard. Refusing to do so, will only set you up for frustration and unhappiness. Use every opportunity possible to create a life that is meaningful and valuable.

No matter who you are, what your background is, where you live or what your economic status is, commitment and effort are requirements for a fulfilled life. It is through consistent work and intentional choices that your personal dreams and visions will be realized.

On the journey to your new life, find persons who have already accomplished goals that are familiar to yours. Doing this eliminates the guesswork, mistakes, and trial and error that you would encounter should you try to blaze your own trail. Take the time to research their methods and learn the steps that they took to get to their success.

On the journey of going after your dreams to create a better life for yourself, you may discover that not everyone is happy to see you succeed. It is so important that you protect your dreams and vision as you go after them. You have to be very careful with whom you share your ideas and plans. Also, ensure that the people close to you are persons who have your best interests at heart and will work with you to bring your dreams to fruition. Persons who have no problem eating up your time and pulling at you often are not good for you. A lot of stress comes from this kind of behavior. It is important that you protect yourself against negative influences.

Develop an emotional barrier against negative influences and establish an atmosphere that can only produce positive and fruitful results. The type of atmosphere you create will determine the kind of life you will have. Work through each day with commitment, diligence, and persistence and never allow your dreams to die. Do everything in your power to guard them, keep them alive and see them manifest.

A happy and wonderful life awaits you if you make the right steps. Through hard work and persistence, you will create a life of fulfillment and joy. Commitment to the plans that you have made, and hard work, will provide you the life that you envision. With determination and diligence, you will become successful! No matter how long it takes, as long as you never give up on your dreams, success will be yours.

Success does not come when there is a lack of commitment and consistency. So often, people expect a quick fix. However, a realistic period of time is necessary before you see your dreams come true.

Sometimes it may take years to see your hard work come to fruition. Many successful people have failed numerous times before seeing the fruit of their labor. Do not get discouraged. If you are consistent, you will notice gradual changes along the way. These changes can increase your motivation, encouraging you to continue and letting you know that you are on the right track.

If you are going to remain consistent in pursuing a good life, you must believe you deserve it. Everyone should feel that he/she deserves the best in life. When you have worked hard and made huge sacrifices to achieve success, you should feel deserving of it. Our positive thoughts and actions draw success to us.

When we put our best foot forth and perform at a level of excellence, we will reap the benefit of our reward. When we succeed through hard work, and persistence, we should feel deserving of our reward. Despite obstacles, flaws and inadequacies along the way, we pressed our way through and should be proud of our achievements. Live a life of giving your all and being your best and believe you deserve the best from life. You deserve to wake up every morning with a sense of accomplishment and happiness. You should feel good about yourself and be excited about the life you have created.

CHAPTER FIFTEEN

Choose To Be Exceptional

*W*e exist in a world in which average is exceptional and slothful is normal. Often, we become comfortable with seeking the path of least resistance, and when the going gets difficult, we have no problem with giving up. In school, when the total grades are averaged together, it's called "grading on the curve." As believers, we cannot allow our standards to be graded by the curve of the world.

No longer are we concerned about being "the lights shining into a world of darkness," and for many, excellence for God has become extinct. We have lowered our standards to those of average persons around us. Many Christians depend on the government rather than on God. Why? We have found it easier to adjust to mediocrity than to the source of excellence: God's Word. Our faith in God has deteriorated dramatically, and so our belief in the God who is "well able" to handle any situation has dwindled to nothing.

I encourage you to determine to be exceptional. Choose to become passionate about fulfilling your life purpose. You are a unique person with a special set of skills. There is no one else with your DNA. This powerful knowledge should invigorate you, motivating you to move from a place of complacency to one of productivity, accomplishment and success.

Perhaps you need to spend time reflecting on your life in order to identify your unique life purpose. Spend time listening to your heart and been honest about the goals you have for yourself. Understanding that having an exceptional life purpose, will help you approach the world with enthusiasm and expectation. Search for ways to expand your abilities and to bring to fruition your dreams and aspirations. Think about how others can benefit from your gifts and talents.

Only you can reveal your life purpose. In the beginning, it may feel uncomfortable to reveal your hopes and dreams. You may be afraid that you may receive criticism or that you may fail. But if you are going to be the exceptional person that you are destined to be, you cannot remain hidden or quiet. Exceptional people take risks, broaden their shoulders and operate with confidence. No one is going to make you exceptional. You have to do that for yourself. No one else in the world can experience your life or fulfill your purpose like you can. Awaken the tiger within you and approach life with strength and vivacity. Choose to be the best that you can be. Choose to be exceptional.

Conclusion

Most people I know have a desire to be exceptional in every area of life. Getting from the point of having a desire, to the point of being exceptional is always the challenge. It is so much easier to think about it, want it or talk about it, than it is to become it. There are steps that must be taken to get to the place of accomplishment.

Becoming an exceptional person takes having a desire, but more than anything, having the willpower to take the necessary steps. Hard work, dedication and consistency are everything when trying to become the best you can in life.

The way you see yourself makes all the difference and will determine your result. Solid focus and having a positive perspective and good attitude will help you overcome whatever challenges you face along the way. Regularly taking the time to reexamine your steps is vital to your success.

As your travel on your road to becoming exceptional, do not allow the spirit of fear to overtake you. Know that you can accomplish all you have set out to. You are on your way to being victorious because you have all the tools you need for success.

You were created to be great and accomplish awesome things. You have the capability and power to become all that you envision. Get started today on the road to becoming EXCEPTIONAL.

YOU WERE BORN TO WIN!

Another **dynamic book** by
Judy L. Smith that will help you
Awaken the champion in you.

ISBN 978-1-4497-2964-6/U.S. $9.95
Westbowpress.com

<u>TO CONTACT DR. JUDY L. SMITH</u>

Judy L. Smith

P. O. Box EE-15051

Nassau, Bahamas

Tel: (242) 362-1350

Email: elderjs242@gmail.com

OR

8000 NW 31st Street

NAS 507, Unit 18

Miami, FL. 33122